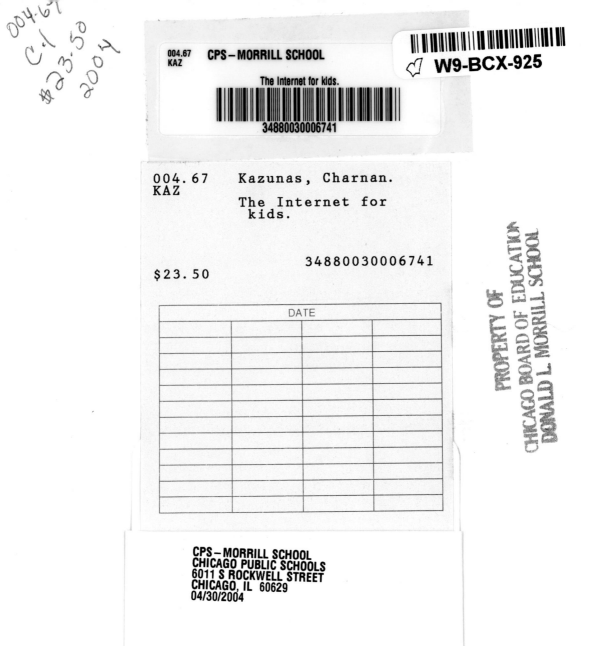

004.67
KAZ

Kazunas, Charnan.

The Internet for
kids.

34880030006741

$23.50

DATE		

W9-BCX-925

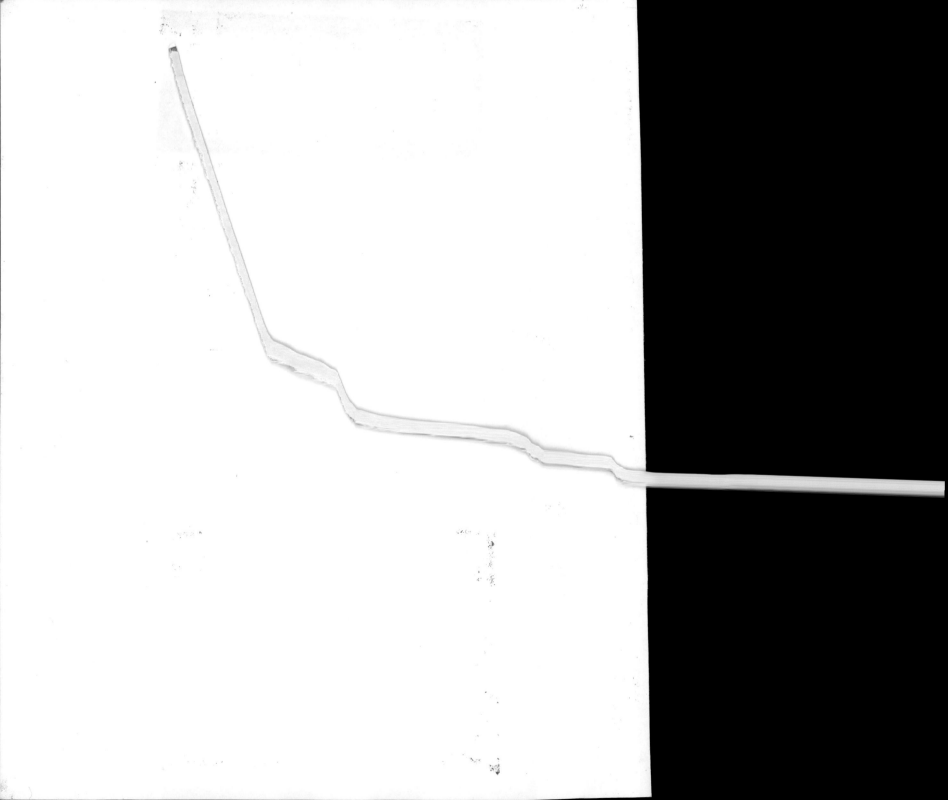

THE INTERNET FOR KIDS

REVISED EDITION

A T R U E **BOOK**

by

**Charnan and
Tom Kazunas**

Children's Press®

A Division of Grolier Publishing

New York London Hong Kong Sydney
Danbury, Connecticut

Find information about the copyright system on the Internet.

Reading Consultant
Linda Cornwell
Learning Resource Consultant
Indiana Department of Education

To my parents, Angie and Al, for their love and support.

Library of Congress Cataloging-in-Publication Data

Kazunas, Charnan.
   The Internet for Kids / by Tom and Charnan Kazunas. — Rev. ed.
     p. cm. — (A true book)
   Includes bibliographical references and index.
   ISBN 0-516-21936-7 (lib. bdg.)   0-516-26857-3 (pbk.)
   1. Internet —Juvenile literature. 2. Computers—Juvenile literature.
[1. Internet. 2. Computers.] I. Kazunas, Thomas. II. Title. III. Series.
TK5105.875.I57K39 2000
004.67'8—dc21   00-060384

Contents

Students are encouraged
to use computers and
the Internet.

Introduction

Over 200 million people around the world used the Internet in 1999. That's the same number of people who live in Canada, England, France, and Italy combined. By 2004, the number of people "online" may reach half a billion. Just what is the Internet?

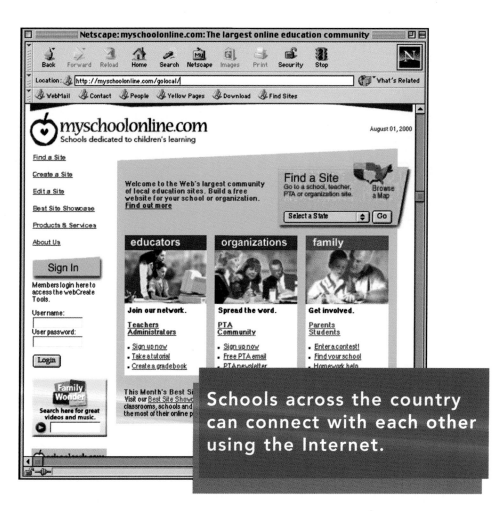

Schools across the country can connect with each other using the Internet.

Who created it? And how can it possibly bring so many people together?

Networks

When two or more computers are connected to each other, they become a network. People who use networked computers can share information with each other, exchange messages, and even run the same programs at the same time on many different computers.

Private networks let businesses, schools, and libraries connect all the computers in their buildings. Networks help factories keep track of their customers' orders. Networks make it easier for schools to record grades, keep attendance records, and plan lunch menus. Networks help people find the books they need when they visit the library.

Computer networks keep track of goods in a warehouse and books in a library.

The Internet

The Internet is like a private network, only much bigger. In fact, the Internet is made up of many different networks combined. Here's how the Internet got its start.

About thirty years ago scientists needed a faster way to share information with each

other. In 1970, four universities connected their computers by telephone for the first time. Even though the schools were in different parts of the United

States, their computers could share information instantly over great distances. The scientists created a special network that connected not only computers in one building, but computers around the world.

This world-wide network became the Internet. Today the Internet is open to the public. It connects more than 134,000 networks, which each contain countless collections of stories, pictures, sounds,

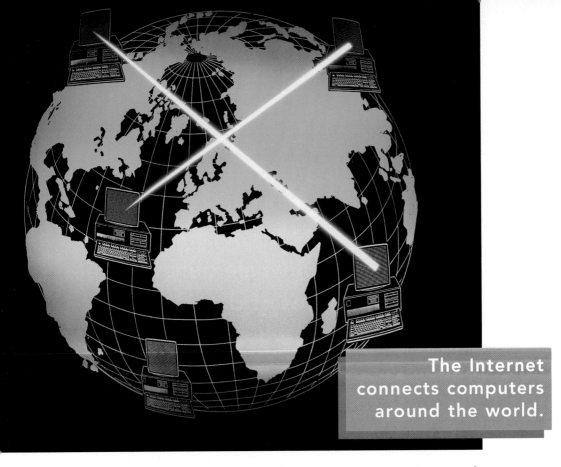

The Internet connects computers around the world.

programs (such as games) and other information. Millions of Americans use their computers to communicate and share information through the Internet.

What's on the Internet?

Imagine you are writing a report on whales. You check out library books as usual, but this time you also use your computer to access the Internet. You might find articles on whale behavior, see photographs and diagrams of different whale species, or study maps of whale migration. You might watch movie clips of whales in action, or even examine 3D computer simulations of whales in motion.

When you're done, you can publish your work on the Internet too.

How It All Works

Computers connected to each other form a network. Networks connected to each other form the Internet. But with all the information available on the Internet, how do you get to what you're looking for?

Each of the thousands of individual networks that make

Servers like the one on the right serve information like a waitress serves food.

up the Internet has set aside
one or more computers to act
as a server. These computer
servers play host to Internet

sites, and serve their information to computer users the way a waiter serves food in a restaurant. And, like a restaurant, each of these servers has its own address. Servers keep track of the addresses of all of the other servers on the Internet, and what sites you will find on them. In a way, every server has a menu—a very long and detailed menu—of all the other servers on the Internet.

Connecting to the Internet

All of these computers and computer networks are connected to each other through telephone lines. That's where the term "online" comes from. You can connect your own computer to the Internet using a telephone line, the right software, and a subscription to either an Internet service provider or an online service.

Internet providers give you access to all the networks on the Internet. Online services, such as America Online, also provide access to the Internet. In addition, they let you play games and use information that you can't get on the Internet.

To find a site on the Internet, you first connect your computer to an Internet server. This server is owned by your Internet provider. When you direct your computer to a particular Internet site, your Internet software will ask this first server to find that site.

Then one server will pass your request on to another and to another, until the address is reached.

Internet Addresses

Internet addresses are called URLs (Uniform Resource Locators). Some look long and confusing, while others are quite short, but they all follow the same simple rules.

The first group of letters on every address tells the network which protocol to use.

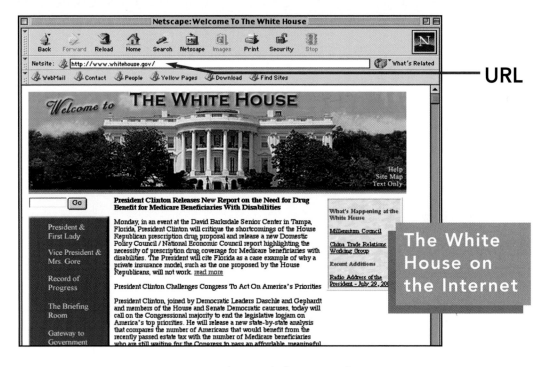

URL

A protocol is like a language—you have to know which one to speak. The most common protocol is **http**, which stands for HyperText Transport Protocol. The protocol is followed by a colon and two slashes (://).

Next comes the domain name. Domain names contain at least two words or phrases, separated by periods. An example would be

www.whitehouse.gov

- **www** means the site is on the World Wide Web.
- **whitehouse** points to a specific server, in this case the server at the White House in Washington, DC.

• the word on the right tells you what kind of site you are visiting. In this example, the address has something to do with the government (that's what "gov" stands for).

To visit the White House server and read about the President, for example, put all the pieces together and enter **http://www.whitehouse.gov**.

The Parts of the Internet

The Internet has several different parts: electronic mail (e-mail), the World Wide Web, chat sessions, Telnet, and Newsgroups are some of the most popular. Each part has a special purpose and way of working.

Write letters and send them through the mail (left). Write e-mail and send it through the Internet (below).

Netscape - [Message Composition]

File   Edit   View   Options   Window

Send   Quote   Attach   Address   Stop

Mail To: Mark
Cc:
Subject: True Books
Attachment:

Hi Mark,

Have you seen the latest True Books? They are excellent!

Your friend,

Allison

E-mail is the simplest use of the Internet. With e-mail you can write an electronic letter on your computer, and send it to another person almost instantly, even if that person is halfway around the world. You can also attach pictures or sounds to an e-mail message.

How does the message get where it is going? An e-mail address is a kind of electronic mail box set up on an Internet server.

Internet Safety

There are a few safety rules that you should follow when you are exploring the Internet. Never give your name, address or phone number to people you don't know. If you are uncomfortable with anything you see or read while online, tell your parents immediately.

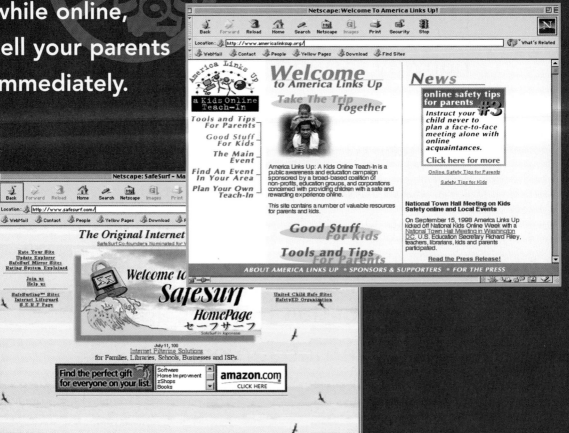

And did you know that computers can catch viruses just like humans? These viruses are a kind of computer program, not a real disease. Ask an adult to check any programs you retrieve from the Internet with "virus detection" software before you use them.

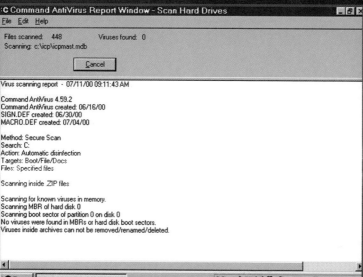

:C Command AntiVirus Report Window – Scan Hard Drives _ ⊟ ×

File Edit Help

Files scanned: 448   Viruses found: 0
Scanning: c:\icp\icpmast.mdb

Cancel

Virus scanning report - 07/11/00 09:11:43 AM

Command AntiVirus 4.59.2
Command AntiVirus created: 06/16/00
SIGN.DEF created: 06/30/00
MACRO.DEF created: 07/04/00

Method: Secure Scan
Search: C:
Action: Automatic disinfection
Targets: Boot/File/Docs
Files: Specified files

Scanning inside .ZIP files

Scanning for known viruses in memory.
Scanning MBR of hard disk 0
Scanning boot sector of partition 0 on disk 0
No viruses were found in MBRs or hard disk boot sectors.
Viruses inside archives can not be removed/renamed/deleted.

Start   Command AntiVir...   N   9:11 AM

E-mail addresses look like this: **jsmith@aol.com**. In this example, "jsmith" is the name of the person who gets the letter. The name is followed by an "at" sign (@), which tells the network that a server name is coming next. In this case "aol.com" is the address for America Online.

The World Wide Web is the newest part of the Internet, and the most popular. The Web brings color,

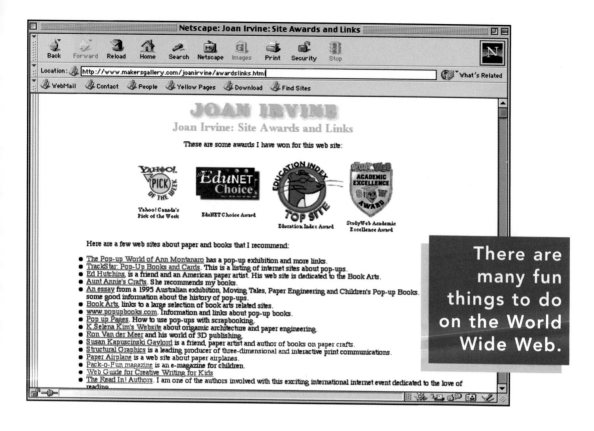

Netscape: Joan Irvine: Site Awards and Links

Location: http://www.makersgallery.com/joanirvine/awardslinks.htm

WebMail   Contact   People   Yellow Pages   Download   Find Sites

JOAN IRVINE

Joan Irvine: Site Awards and Links

These are some awards I have won for this web site:

Yahoo! Canada's
Pick of the Week

EduNET Choice Award

Education Index Award

StudyWeb Academic
Excellence Award

Here are a few web sites about paper and books that I recommend:

- The Pop-up World of Ann Montanaro has a pop-up exhibition and more links.
- TrackStar: Pop-Up Books and Cards. This is a listing of internet sites about pop-ups.
- Ed Hutchins, is a friend and an American paper artist. His web site is dedicated to the Book Arts.
- Aunt Annie's Crafts. She recommends my books.
- An essay from a 1995 Australian exhibition, Moving Tales, Paper Engineering and Children's Pop-up Books. some good information about the history of pop-ups.
- Book Arts, links to a large selection of book arts related sites.
- www.popupbooks.com. Information and links about pop-up books.
- Pop up Pages. How to use pop-ups with scrapbooking.
- K Selena Kim's Website about origamic architecture and paper engineering.
- Ron Van der Meer and his world of 3D publishing.
- Susan Kapuscinski Gaylord is a friend, paper artist and author of books on paper crafts.
- Structural Graphics is a leading producer of three-dimensional and interactive print communications.
- Paper Airplane is a web site about paper airplanes.
- Pack-o-Fun magazine is an e-magazine for children.
- Web Guide for Creative Writing for Kids
- The Read In! Authors. I am one of the authors involved with this exciting international internet event dedicated to the love of reading.

There are many fun things to do on the World Wide Web.

moving pictures and sound to your computer screen. When you're done looking at one Web page, click on a short-cut called a hyperlink to whisk off to other Web pages.

Search and

Browser software lets you "surf the Net" by jumping from one Web page to another. But what if you need specific information? Jumping around on the Web can be like looking through a file drawer for one sheet of paper—or through many file drawers.

Retrieval Tools

The Internet's file drawer is huge! There are 17 million sites on the World Wide Web and they contain one billion pages of information.

Fortunately, many "search engine" sites, such as Alta Vista, are available on the Web to help you find information. And some sites, called meta-search engines, will even search the search engines.

File   Edit   Go To   Mail   Members   Window   Help

People in Room:
15

ANDUP05
MBarron02
Sportsfguy
Prplcrayon
JOKER284
SPiffyest
YTCC Mac
SavageJolt

Rooms   Preferences   Help & Info   Youth Tech

YTCC Mac:	Wow, Edge719--I never do that well in Math. What are you in now? Algebra II?
YTCC Mac:	Welcome to the Youth Tech Chat, Prplcrayon!
Edge719:	i'm taking course II math
YTCC Mac:	Edge719, everyone has a weakness, I guess.
SavageJolt:	ya YTCC I'd like to see u flunk high school and still get a well paying job
YTCC Mac:	SavageJolt, the important thing is to always try your best. :-)
OnlineHost:	Sportsfguy has entered the room.
OnlineHost:	Sportsfguy has entered the room.
OnlineHost:	MBarron02 has entered the room.
YTCC Mac:	Welcome to the Youth Tech Chat, Sportsfguy!
YTCC Mac:	Glad you could come back, Sportsfguy!
YTCC Mac:	That's all you can do.
YTCC Mac:	Welcome back, MBarron02!
MBarron02:	anybody out there
Sportsfguy:	y
Sportsfguy:	yes
YTCC Mac:	MBarron02, have you seen KEYWORD: ORIENTATION EXPRESS?
Byblndr:	im out here
OnlineHost:	ANDUP05 has entered the room.
OnlineHost:	ANDUP05 has entered the room.
MBarron02:	wanna chat

Just like a discussion in a classroom (opposite), on-line chat sessions (left) can include several different people.

Chat sessions let you
"talk" to people all over the
world. You type in a message
and instantly it is sent to all
the other people tuned into

your chat group. Someone answers back, you send another message, and before you know it, you're having a "conversation" with people all around the world.

Telnet lets distant computers connect to each other and run each other's programs. If your public library uses Telnet, you can hook your computer into the library's system to find and reserve the book you want.

Netscape: LEO Via Telnet

Back | Forward | Reload | Home | Search | Netscape | Images | Print | Security | Stop

Netsite: http://www.nypl.org/catalogs/telnet.html

WebMail | Contact | People | Yellow Pages | Download | Find Sites

The New York Public Library | **The Branch Libraries**

| Home | Catalogs | Digital Library | Electronic Resources | The Libraries | Search the Internet |

Connect to LEO via Telnet   At the login prompt type: **leo** (lower case only).

About Telnet Software

LEO maybe accessed using Telnet. If you have a properly configured Telnet application on your computer, selecting th _via Telnet"_ button should automatically launch a Telnet session. _Some on-line services do not currently support telnet a_

Please contact your Internet service provider (ISP) with questions concerning Telnet support, and how to obtain and configure Telnet.

Here is an outline of the steps involved in setting up Telnet access if your computer is not currently configured to do so.

1. Obtain Telnet software that is compatible with your operating system. There are several freely downloadable Telnet programs available through the Internet. Contact your Internet service provider for recommended applications.

2. Install the Telnet program so that it runs on your computer. If you download a Telnet program from the Internet you will need to run the file you downloaded.

3. Using your Web browser (Internet Explorer, Netscape...) preferences or setup, enable the Telnet program to run with your browser.

MM/CMB 06/01/2000

With Telnet, you can use a library's catalog in your home.

37

File   Edit   Special   Group   Article   View   Window   Help

Looking for childrens book authors, by Mad C Mike, 11 Dec 1996 15:41:10 GMT   1 of 88

interport.announce
interport.nyc
interport.questions
interport.www
rec.arts.books.childrens
rec.sport.cricket.info

Mary Ann Lavandero	9	Tickle Me-Elmo
Ettinger/Weder	6	WTB: Boys' Sports Juveniles, particularly Baseball
Steven Cieluch	141	FS: Children's & Illustrated Holiday books
Laurie Campbell	25	Re: Yet another book ID question
Artejay4U	9	Our Children's Art
Id1952@aol.com	3	Re: WTB Walt Disney Spin & Marty [Whitman]
Caroline Tosswill	19	ABRADACABRA!
Jennifer Slegg	15	Laura Ingalls Wilder Mailing List
JimGore	9	FS: Nancy Drew Books, $6 ppd. Each
JimGore	6	Baseball Players Do Amazing Things FS
Pendragon Books	25	FS: WINIFRED FINLAY
Umnak	9	bill grogan's goat
The Dix	37	Re: Know "Bill Grogan's Goat" lyrics?
Umnak	5	Nash Book Wanted
John Sievers	5	FS: Story Number 1 by Eugene Ionesco
Jesse Martin	5	FS: Maida
Jesse Martin	3	Stig of the Dump
Deborah Gascoyne	12	Re: Title Changes
NaughtyZut	5	Re: WAIT TILL HELEN COMES-like books
JimGore	6	A Campfire Girl's Chum by Jane L. Stewart FS

| << | >> | View/list | Format | Skip all | Post | Follow | Reply | Archive | Extract |

Newsgroups are like magazines— there's one for every interest.

Newsgroups are electronic discussion groups. In such a group, people around the world "discuss" a subject, like in a chat session. Only, instead of talking at the same time, members of a newsgroup post messages on electronic bulletin boards. Anyone "subscribing" to the newsgroup can then read these messages and leave their own message in reply.

Use a newsgroup to exchange information about Dalmation puppies.

For example, if you and your friends like Dalmatian puppies, you could set up a newsgroup for everyone who likes Dalmatians—if there isn't one already. You can then share your knowledge and questions all around the world. Eventually, thousands of people might subscribe.

The Future of the Internet

People already have thousands of uses for the Internet, but new ideas and new inventions keep coming. You no longer need a desktop computer to connect to the Internet—a wireless telephone can now display tomorrow's forecast from the Weather Channel.

Surprising new Internet devices will contain tiny, dime-size computers called "embedded systems." They will connect to the Internet and let a Web-enabled picture frame receive and display snap shots of your newborn cousin. They will send your grandfather's doctor a report on his health—from his wristwatch.

Few people predicted that in less than ten years the

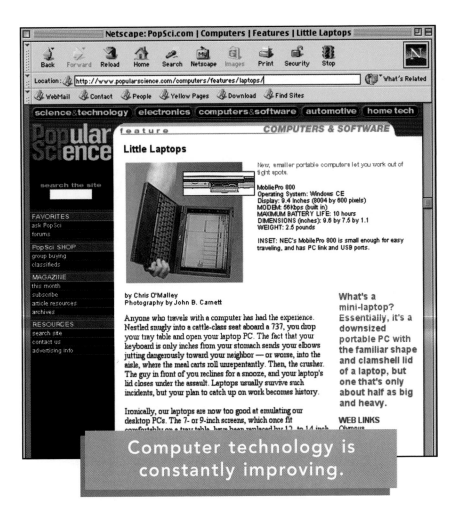

Computer technology is constantly improving.

World Wide Web would become a world-wide wonder. The next ten years will be amazing!

To Find Out More

Here are some additional resources to help you learn more about the Internet:

Books

Brimner, Larry Dane. **The World Wide Web.** Children's Press, 2000.

Gralla, Preston. **On-Line Kids: A Young Surfer's Guide to Cyberspace.** John Wiley & Sons, 1999.

Pedersen, Ted, and Francis Moss. **Internet for Kids: A Beginner's Guide to Surfing the Net.** Price Stern Sloan, 1997.

Salzman, Marian, and Robert Pondisco. **Kids On-Line.** Avon Books, 1995.

Internet Sites

Just for Kids
http://www.foodtips.com/ kids/

Links to Internet sites like NASA, Sports Illustrated for Kids, and Smithsonian Magazine's Kids' Castle.

Sea World/Busch Gardens Animal Information Database
http://www.seaworld.org/ infobook.html

Find information on aardvarks to zebras and hear the sounds they make at the Animal Sounds Library.

Seussville
http://www.randomhouse.com/seussville/

This is the official Dr. Seuss site, with quizzes, contests, activities, and an "Ask the Cat-in-the-Hat" feature.

Nickelodeon
http://www.nick.com

Listen to music, play games, and learn about your favorite Nick shows.

The White House
http://www.whitehouse.gov

Take a tour of the most famous residence in the world. A look at its occupants as well as the building.

Yahooligans
http://www.yahooligans.com

The best place to begin a search for kid stuff on the net.

Important Words

browser a program used to look at World Wide Web pages on the Internet

hypertext words or phrases in an Internet document that connect to another document

network a collection of computers that share information and programs

protocol a set of rules computers follow to communicate and share information

server a computer and software that manages the flow of information on a computer network

URL Universal Resource Locator; the address of a World Wide Web page

World Wide Web the part of the Internet using graphics and hypertext that connects addresses and allows you to move between them easily.

Index

Meet the Authors

Charnan Simon and Tom Kazunas are married and live in Madison, Wisconsin, with their daughters, Ariel and Hana, their dog Sam, and their two computers.

Tom's computer is new and fast and powerful. Tom uses it to solve complicated math problems, design books, visit websites, do research, and play all kinds of games.

Charnan's computer is old and slow and tired. Every morning when she turns it on, it says "Disk boot failure." This means Charnan has time to walk the dog, make a cup of tea, and write a postcard to a friend. By then her computer is warmed up, and Charnan can get to work writing books.

Photographs ©: Christine Osinski: 1, 28 center, 32 inset, 38; Monkmeyer Press: 26 top (Peter Glass), 19 top (Goodwin), 32 (Kagan), 14 (McCutcheon), 19 middle right (Wolf); PhotoEdit: 4 (Spencer Grant); Photo Researchers: 13 (Tony Craddock/SPL), 37 (Laima Druskis), 9 right, 17 (Jeff Greenberg), 8 (David M. Grossman), 40 (Jerry Irwin), 11, 34, (Will & Deni McIntyre), 29 (Oliver Meckes/EOS), 17 (David Parker), 9 left (Lee F. Snyder).